Written by Kelly Hanson
Illustrated by Paula Zimmerschied

Barnyard Book

Written By: Kelly Hanson
Illustrated By: Paula Zimmerschied
Copyright 2014

Published by: Sophic Pursuits, Inc.

All rights reserved. No part of this book may be used or reproduced in any manner without written permission of the author and publisher.

Publisher's Cataloging-in-Publication Data
Hanson, Kelly, 1969-
      Barnyard Book

      Illustrated By: Paula Zimmerschied

ISBN 978-1-940843-05-6
JUVENILE NONFICTION/Animals/Farm Animals

THE FARM AND THE BARNYARD

Have you ever eaten scrambled eggs and bacon? Have you ever thrown a football or played catch with a baseball? Maybe you've worn a knit cap or even chewed bubble gum. None of these things would be possible if it were not for the farmer and the barnyard. Today, it is estimated that one farmer can provide enough food and fiber for 155 people for a year. The food they provide is more than just corn and carrots. They provide us with steak, hamburger, sausage and chicken nuggets. Being a farmer is not just a job. It is a way of life. Everyday starts with the cock-a-doodle-do of the rooster and ends in the comfort of the farmhouse. All the hours in between are filled with chores and a great deal of hard work. It has been that way for hundreds of years. In all that time, the tools and machinery have changed, but not the need to tend to the crops and animals.

THE FARMHOUSE

The term farmhouse refers to the main house on a farm. A pioneer farm, in the early to middle 1800's, consisted of about 50 acres of land, the farmhouse, a barn and several outbuildings. By the 1900's, the average farm had expanded to over 120 acres.

Living on the farm meant the farmer and his family could begin work bright and early usually at or before daybreak. His wife, after finishing her indoor chores, would help tend the garden and work in the fields.

The farmhouse was built to be functional and was often well-stocked with food and daily necessities. These houses were well-crafted and sturdy. The typical farmhouse was two-stories, had white wood siding and a dirt road leading to them. The roof was usually gabled with the front pitch extending out over the porch, which was and is the most important feature of a farmhouse. Many farmers enjoyed quiet hours with their families on the big porch. Many farmhouses had a cellar below the front of the house for storing bottled and canned food. Root cellars were on the backside of the house and used for storing dry goods like potatoes and onions.

Inside the farmhouse, a stone fireplace, often used burning coal and corncobs, heated the home. The farmer's wife would cook in cast iron cookware over the open hearth. Formal areas were generally positioned at the front of the house and areas designated for chores were at the back. Chores for the farmer's wife included spinning wool into yarn, quilting, and making soap and candles. She also spent many hours cooking and canning.

The farmer's wife also had to wash the clothes. Water was either hand carried into the house or a hand pump delivered rainwater stored in the cistern. The farmer's wife did all this without electricity. In the evenings and early mornings, the light in the farmhouse was provided by kerosene lamps. After the clothes were washed and dried, the farmer's wife had to iron them with a heavy iron which was filled with hot coals.

The farmhouse often grew as the family grew. A typical family would have been the farmer and his wife plus their children, their grandchildren, a niece or nephew and perhaps a farm worker or two. Having 10 or more people living in the farmhouse was common. Out buildings would be built on large farms to house the workers. Of course, guests and travelers were welcome and were provided a place to sleep. It was common for travelers to spend the night on the porch.

The farmhouse is essential to a no-nonsense and hard-working way of life.

THE FARMER

The farmers who grow crops like corn, wheat, soybeans, beets and potatoes are called crop farmers. Farmers who raise animals like pigs and cows are called livestock or dairy farmers and those who raise chickens are called poultry farmers.

Crop farmers have the responsibility of deciding what to plant and when to plant. They have to make certain the soil is rich in nutrients (fertilized) to ensure a healthy crop. They have to till the soil and plant the seeds. Crop farmers then have to monitor the growing plants for insects and other pests. On smaller farms, scarecrows help keep away birds that eat the seeds or the crops. When the crops are ripe, the farmer harvests, packages, stores and then sells what he has grown.

Many farmers grow a combination of crops like corn and beans, wheat and asparagus, or cotton and barley. This helps ensure that if a crop fails because of bad weather or disease, the other crop will still be good for harvesting.

During the growing and harvesting seasons, crop farmers usually work from sunrise to sunset. During the winter, they plan for the spring planting and repair their tools.

Livestock, dairy and poultry farmers are responsible for the daily feeding and caring for their animals all year. Dairy cows must be milked every day. The farmers also maintain the barn, coops, pens, fences and other farm buildings. Choosing which animals to send to market is the farmer's choice. It is an important decision because the animals have to be the right weight to get the most value for his animals. Additionally, the farmer chooses which animals to breed to produce the best offspring. And just when all the chores are almost finished…there is all that poop to scoop.

Farm work can be dangerous. Tractors and other farm machinery can cause serious injury so it is necessary to pay attention and be alert while working. Modern machines like tractors and combines make the work easier than in the days before gasoline engines. In the olden days, farmers would use their animals, oxen and draft horses, to pull plows and wagons. Believe it or not, some farmers still prefer working animals to machines.

Farming is hard work, but farmers enjoy working outdoors and making a living off the land. Most farmers work for themselves and relish the independence and living in a rural area (the country).

The farmers of pioneer farms in the early and middle 1800's, farmed approximately 50 acres. They used oxen to plow the fields because they were stronger than horses and didn't require grain. Horses, however, were more agile and once the farm was established, the farmer would trade in his oxen for horses. Typically, those horses were draft horses like Percherons or Belgians.

By the 1900's, the farmer began using cast iron and steel tools to work the farm. Additionally, he built corn cribs, hog houses, chicken houses, machine sheds and the all important…outhouses. The farmer, by this time, had a working windmill and water pump.

Chores were easier for the farmer's wife, too. Although the days of traveling to the local mercantile to purchase a new shirt or a pair pants were still in the future, she didn't have to hand sew her family's clothes. She could purchase a treadle-sewing machine.

The farmer and his family spent most of their time on the farm. Farming was their way of life. More crops and more animals meant the farmer could sell them for money. The money was used to purchase items that he couldn't grow or make. Store bought and mail order items were a luxury. Even trips into town were considered special. The entire family would take a break from the daily routine of chores and venture into town for a well-earned Sunday outing.

DOG (*Canis lupus familiaris*)

Female Dog: Bitch	**Male Dog:** Dog
Baby Dog: Puppy	**Group:** Pack, Kennel
Sound: Bark	

Dogs eat dog food, both dry and canned. They also eat meat and vegetables, including grass. Dogs love peanut butter, chicken, fish, cheese and, of course, dog treats. They will eat just about anything. Unfortunately, sometimes they eat things that make them sick; things like chocolate and grapes. Sometimes salmon, onions, garlic, macadamia nuts and turkey skin can cause health problems for dogs. Any sugar-free item containing Xylitol should never be given to dogs.

Typically, a dog lives between 8 to 15 years. The breed and lifestyle can make a tremendous impact on the longevity. The general rule of thumb is that the larger the breed of dog the shorter the life span. Smaller breeds tend to live from 12 to 15 years and the larger breeds live about 10 years. There are exceptions. It is not unusual to hear of a feisty large breed living to 15 years or a small breed making it to 20 years. The record holding oldest dog, an Australian Cattle Dog named Bluey, lived for 29 years and 5 months.

After breeding, a dog will give birth in 63 days. The number of puppies in a litter varies based on breed. An average estimation of a litter is anywhere from 3 to 6, but 10 puppies aren't uncommon. A Napoleon Mastiff holds the record for largest litter: 24 puppies!

Farmers use dogs to help herd and protect livestock, and kill vermin. Dogs are also used to help hunters flush out and to retrieve game birds. The kind of work needed to be performed has determined the size and shape of dogs. Smaller breeds, like terriers, are used to "go to ground" meaning they dig and burrow into rodent tunnels. Larger breeds like collies and shepherds herd and protect sheep and cows. Retrievers and pointers help hunters in the woods and marshes. Other dogs are used to pull wagons and sleds. Farm dogs also keep a watchful eye on the barnyard. They know it is their territory and responsibility to keep all things in order. They use their amazing sense of smell to sniff out any visitor be they welcome (farm friends, family and guests) or unwelcome (foxes, bobcats or rats). Farm dogs are good workers and faithful companions.

Border Collies have helped shepherds gather their sheep. They are highly intelligent and definitely need a job. Collies and Old English Sheepdogs are excellent herders and watchdogs. They are used to tend to the flocks and protect them from predators. Old English Sheepdogs do well in cold weather so they are perfect to herd reindeer. Miniature Schnauzers are excellent rat killers and Blue Heelers specialize in driving cattle.

FUN FACTS ABOUT DOGS:

🐾 Dogs have twice as many muscles for moving their ears than people. Their sense of hearing is more than ten times more acute than a human's.

🐾 Dogs only sweat from their feet. Their sweat glands are between the paw pads. A dog's nose helps keep him cool. Panting is their way of turning on the air conditioner; the longer the nose, the better his cooling system.

🐾 All dogs are identical in anatomy - 321 bones and 42 permanent teeth.

🐾 Dogs naturally like to play keep-away better than fetch.

🐾 Not all dogs are born swimmers. Some dogs need to be encouraged to swim. Some breeds are more natural swimmers than others. Basset Hounds can't swim.

🐾 People have kept dogs as pets for over 12, 000 years!

CAT (*Felis catus*)

Female Cat: Queen	**Male Cat:** Tomcat
Baby Cat: Kitten	**Group:** Clowder, Pounce
	Group of Kittens: Kindle, Litter, Intrigue
Sound: Mew, Purr	

The farmer classically allows a feral cat to claim the barn as its home. The cat earns its keep by ridding the barn and surrounding yard of nuisance pests.

Cats eat dry or moist cat food. They also eat mice, rats, lizards, grasshoppers, fish, birds, spiders and frogs. Mother Nature designed cats to obtain most of their water from their diet of normal prey animals. The barn cats are usually provided just enough food to ensure their survival. They have a job to do and if the farmer feeds them too well, then they might not do what's expected of them: eat the mice and rats that live in the barn. Barn cats are good hunters and have excellent night vision, which is why they usually hunt at dusk, during the night and dawn.

Even though cats are good hunters, they miss their prey about 2 of every 3 tries. A house cat's typical meal of cat food is about the same as 5 mice for a barn cat.

Daylight hours are spent lying in the warmth of the sunbeam. A cat can sleep 16 to 18 hours a day, but even though asleep, they are still alert to what's going on around them.

If providing tap water to a cat, let the water sit for about 24 hours before giving it to a cat. The tap water contains chlorine, which irritates the sensitive parts of a cat's nose. Letting it sit awhile will allow the chlorine to dissipate.

Typically a cat lives 12-15 years. Indoor cats tend to live longer and have been known to live well into their 20's. One cat, Baby, is said to have lived to be 37 years old! Outdoor cats or barn cats generally don't live as long. They lead a more hazardous life than that of a pampered indoor cat. Barn cats face dangers like tractors, farm machinery, and other predators like coyotes, owls and bobcats. Sometimes they tangle with poisonous creatures like spiders and snakes that fight back.

After breeding, the queen will give birth to an average litter of 4 kittens in about 65 days. A queen can have 2 or 3 litters a year. Over her lifetime, she may be the mother to well over 100 kittens.

The kittens are born blind, deaf and helpless. Their eyes open between 8 to 10 days old and are always blue at birth. After a few months, the final color of the eye will set. It takes 9 days for their ear canals to open. They depend on their mother until they are about 6 weeks old. Cats reach maturity between 9 and 10 months of age. It is not uncommon for a feral (a cat with little or no human contact) cat to seek out a barn or farmhouse porch to have her babies. With humans around, there is less chance of predators that could harm the newborns.

? ? ? ? ? ? ? ? ? ? ? ? ? ?

Did you know? Cats have over one hundred vocal sounds, while dogs have about ten.

? ? ? ? ? ? ? ? ? ? ? ? ? ?

White cats with blue eyes are typically deaf. Deafness seems to depend on the blue eye because a white cat with only one blue eye will be deaf only in the ear on the blue eye side. Luckily, white cats with orange eyes are not afflicted.

Farmers use barn cats to rid the barns of mice and rats. Rodents destroy insulation, electrical wiring, bedding, and leather. They eat the grain intended for livestock or for the market. By hunting mice, cats save farmers up to 10 tons of grain every year.

Rodents also can be infested with parasites or diseases that are harmful to other animals and to humans. Even rodent droppings (poop) can cause illness. Barn cats that eat these animals will need preventive health care and farmers comply. An old farming saying is "Take care of your animals and they will take care of you."

Cats are excellent climbers and jumpers. To determine how high a cat can jump, just look at its tail. A cat can jump 7 times as high as its tail is long.

Cats have excellent hearing. Their hearing is much more sensitive than humans or dogs. They have 32 muscles that control their outer ears (humans only have 6) that allows them to rotate their ears 180 degrees. They can turn their ears toward a sound 10 times faster than the best watchdog.

? ? ? ? ? ? ? ? ? ? ? ? ? ?

Did you know? A cat's whiskers are extremely sensitive to the slightest touch. They are used for testing obstacles and sensing changes in the environment. In darkness, a cat can feel its way by using its whiskers.

? ? ? ? ? ? ? ? ? ? ? ? ? ?

WATER

All plants and animals require water to grow and survive. Imagine what your day would be like if there were no water available. How would you wash your face or brush your teeth without water? On a hot summer day, there would be no tall glass of ice water. Did you know your body is made up of mostly water? It's true. Without water, life wouldn't be possible. Since water is so important, obtaining it and storing it is critical to life on a farm.

THE WINDMILL AND CISTERN

The windmill on the farm serves a vital function as a pump to move water from the cistern to areas where it is needed. Some farms have a large cistern built above ground.

A cistern is a large tank used for holding water, specifically rainwater. Similar to a well, the cistern ensures the water is not contaminated and does not evaporate. Typically, a cistern is round or rectangular and has a cover to keep insects, plants or animals away from the water.

Cisterns come in various shapes and sizes. Anything that stores water for later use can be called a cistern, even a large jar. The tank on the back of your toilet can be called a cistern!

The windmill harnesses the power of the wind to bring the water up from the cistern to pipes that are above ground.

The farmer would then attach more pipes and hoses to allow the water to travel out to the fields to irrigate the crops and to the corrals for watering the animals. The pipes might even end up in the farm house kitchen. Perhaps you have seen a sink that uses a hand pump rather than a faucet. It only takes a few minutes of hand pumping to get the water flowing.

The farm wind pump was invented in 1854 by Daniel Halliday. Eventually, the wood tower and blades were upgraded to steel and by 1930, there were over 600,000 windmills in use in the Midwest. There aren't as many today as they have been replaced by electric pumps. Mr. Halliday's invention helped the development of the western two-thirds of the United States. The early settlers faced hard times, but the new technology helped them shape their environment by bringing water to dry areas to allow for the possibility of farming and ranching.

Between 1854 and 1920, there were over 700 companies manufacturing windmills. Unfortunately, only two of those companies are left. Most of the old windmills have been purchased by private collectors or museums.

Windmills still have value in areas where electricity is not available. Plus, many people who want to help the environment and "go green" are returning to windmills as an alternative energy source. People nowadays use windmills because the wind is free. They don't require much work and as long as they are maintained, the windmill will continue to pump water to the crops and livestock for a very long time.

Windmills, in addition to pumping water for crops and livestock, are used to keep ponds healthy and mosquito free. The moving water reduces bacteria build-up and replenishes oxygen levels. A healthy lake or pond is an excellent environment for fish. Windmills can be found working at fish hatcheries.

The crop farmer focus on plants. A particular plant that is vital to humans and to livestock is corn. As important as storing water, storing crops, especially corn, has been of concern to the farmer.

CORN CRIB

Corn cribs began popping up on farms around 1701, as a structure in which to store Indian maize. Corn cribs were commonly built on wooden or stone posts high above the ground and the overhanging eaves helped prevent rain from splashing inside. By 1860, the distinctive shape of slanted walls with wooden slats was typical. The spaces between the slats allow for air to circulate and help keep the corn dry. Building the corn crib on the high posts also helps keep out rodents.

Corn cribs primarily serve as storage buildings for corn. Large farms had several smaller cribs rather than one large crib. Corn cribs stored shelled corn, corn on the cobs and the cobs. Cobs were used for kindling and for smoking meat. They were even used as toilet paper! Can you imagine?

The earliest American barns were actually corn cribs which were built large enough for a wagon to be driven inside.

Corn cribs can also be used to store a variety of items besides corn. A farmer can use his crib to store firewood or barnyard equipment. Corn cribs can also be used to house ducks and geese at night to protect them from predators like foxes and raccoons. Some farmers have even turned their corn cribs into dog kennels.

Corn is a valuable crop and all parts of the plant are used. The leaves and stalks, called fodder, and kernels are used as animal feed. Humans also consume the kernels. Have you ever eaten creamed corn, corn on the cob or popcorn? Corn flakes, grits, corn bread and corn chips all contain corn. Corn syrup is found in a variety of candy bars. Corn starch is found in a variety of products. Wallpaper paste and automobile tires are just two. Corn starch can be used in numerous ways. You can give your dog a bath just using corn starch, no water needed. Just rub it on and brush it out. No need to buy glue when corn starch is around. Mix with water and you've got yourself homemade paste. How about paint? Mix ¼ cup cornstarch and 2 cups cold water and bring to a boil. Boil until thick, remove and pour into a small container. Add desired food coloring and PRESTO….homemade finger paints!

Bundles of stalks make excellent insulation for animal quarters. The more densely packed the bundles, the warmer the animals will be. The stalks can also be ground up and used as compost to help fertilize the soil.

The shucks can be used as stuffing for mattresses. They also can be used to make brooms and chair seats. In addition to a fuel source, the cobs can be carved into pipes. Can you imagine Frosty the Snowman without a corn-cob pipe? Corn cobs are very absorbent and can be found in items like fertilizers, vitamins, hand soaps, cosmetics and kitty litter.

? ? ? ? ? ? ? ? ? ? ? ? ? ?

Did you know?
There are over 2,500 products that use corn in some form during the production or processing?

? ? ? ? ? ? ? ? ? ? ? ? ? ?

Why not make CORNBREAD MUFFINS?
Here's a recipe just for you.

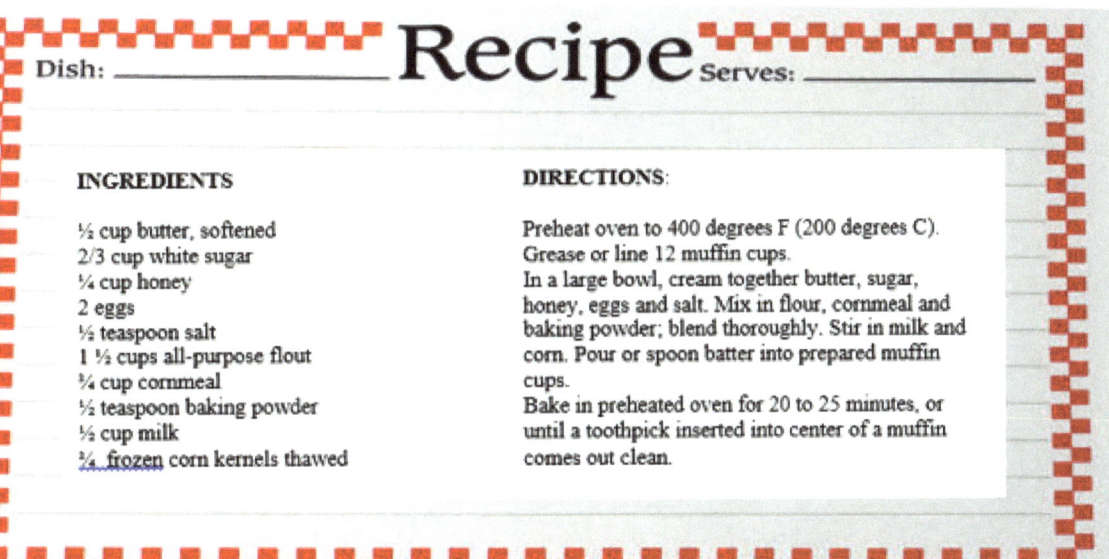

Dish: _____ **Recipe** **Serves:** _____

INGREDIENTS

½ cup butter, softened
2/3 cup white sugar
¼ cup honey
2 eggs
½ teaspoon salt
1 ½ cups all-purpose flour
¾ cup cornmeal
½ teaspoon baking powder
½ cup milk
¾ frozen corn kernels thawed

DIRECTIONS:

Preheat oven to 400 degrees F (200 degrees C). Grease or line 12 muffin cups.
In a large bowl, cream together butter, sugar, honey, eggs and salt. Mix in flour, cornmeal and baking powder; blend thoroughly. Stir in milk and corn. Pour or spoon batter into prepared muffin cups.
Bake in preheated oven for 20 to 25 minutes, or until a toothpick inserted into center of a muffin comes out clean.

APPLE TREE *(Malus domestica)*

When you learned the alphabet, what was the first letter you learned? Do you remember what that letter was? A is for Apple.

October is National Apple Month.

Apples grow on trees and a group of apple trees growing together is called an apple orchard. An apple tree grows to at least 20 feet tall. The dwarf trees grow to about 10 feet tall and produce fruit earlier than standard-size trees. It is also easier to pick the apples from short trees. Imagine trying to pick apples from tall trees? You definitely would need a ladder!

? ? ? ? ? ? ? ? ? ? ? ? ? ? ?

***Did you know?** The largest apple picked weighed three pounds!*

? ? ? ? ? ? ? ? ? ? ? ? ? ? ?

Apple trees need direct sunlight for proper growth and good quality apples. Early morning sun is essential because it dries the morning dew off of the leaves. Damp leaves can lead to disease.

In the spring, when the apple flowers bloom, honey bees and other insects pollinate the flowers. Where the flower blooms, an apple will grow. If there weren't any bees or other insects, then there would be no apples and that would be a sad situation.

Apples ripen on the outside branches first. Because apples can bruise, picking them has to be done with care. There is a proper method to picking apples. It's done by twisting the stem until it breaks. Pulling straight down only harms the tree. There is no need to shake the tree branches either. Once picked, the apples are gently placed into a special apple picking basket. The apple basket has no bottom. It is held closed by a buckle that when released will cause the apples to roll out the bottom and into a bushel basket or crate. A good rule of thumb about handling apples is to handle them as if they were eggs.

Apples are grown in all 50 states in 2,500 varieties. Throughout the world, there are 7,500 different varieties of apples.

? ? ? ? ? ? ? ? ? ? ? ? ? ? ?

***Did you know?** Apples come in all shades of reds, greens, and yellows.*

? ? ? ? ? ? ? ? ? ? ? ? ? ? ?

The apple tree originated in Europe and Asia between the Caspian Sea and the Black Sea. The ancient Greeks and Romans considered the apple a favorite fruit. North America didn't have apples until the pilgrims planted the first tree in the Massachusetts Bay Colony. In those days, apples were called winter bananas or melt-in-your-mouths.

On September 26, 1774, a man named John Chapman was born in Massachusetts. He wanted apple trees everywhere so no one would go hungry. He started apple orchards in Illinois, Indiana, Kentucky, Pennsylvania and Ohio. Even now, some of those trees still bear apples. Because he loved apples and loved planting them, he earned the nickname of Johnny Appleseed. He spent 49 years of his life in the American wilderness planting apple seeds.

Apples are measured by pecks and bushels. It takes 4 pecks to make a bushel. A peck weighs about 10-14 pounds and a bushel of apples weighs about 42-48 pounds. Eight medium sized apples weigh just over 2 pounds and will make one 9-inch apple pie or three cups of apple sauce.

Apples ripen 6-10 times faster at room temperature than if they are refrigerated. Kept cool, fresh-picked apples will keep for weeks. The variety, however, does make a difference. Red and Yellow Delicious don't keep very long. Freezing an apple will rupture all of its cells and cause it to turn into one large bruise overnight.

Can you name some items made with apples? Apple juice, apple sauce, apple butter, apple dumpling, apple pie, apple strudel, apple cider, and caramel apples are just a few examples of what people can make with apples.

PUMPKIN

The pumpkin is native to North America and can be dated back to 7000- 5500 B.C. The name "pumpkin" originated from a Greek word "pepon" meaning large melon and that is exactly what a pumpkin is. Record holding pumpkins easily weigh over 1,000 pounds!

Native American Indians called the pumpkin "isqoutm squash" and ate them as a staple in their diet. The pumpkin is rich in vitamin A, vitamin C, and potassium. The Indians would roast long strips of pumpkin in the open fire and eat them. The seeds were used for food and medicine. The Native American Indians also dried strips and wove them into mats. Even the pumpkin flowers are edible. During colonial times, the pumpkin was an ingredient in pie crusts…but NOT the filling!

When early settlers came to North America, the Indians shared the pumpkin and soon the colonists accepted the pumpkins as a staple in their diet. There are many recipes using pumpkins in dessert, stews, soups and bread. Then there is the favorite: Pumpkin Pie. The origin of the pumpkin pie is thought to have occurred when colonists sliced off the top, removed the seeds, filled the pumpkin with milk, spices and honey and then baked in the hot ashes of a dying fire. Yummy!

Pumpkins grow all over the world with one exception. Antarctica is the only continent where pumpkins won't grow.

To have pumpkins ready by Halloween, the seeds need to be planted in late May or early June. Pumpkins need full sun and lots of room to grow. They should be planted in rows that are 4 to 6 feet apart. Plant 2 seeds in each hole and each hole about 2 feet apart. Once the seedlings have 3 or 4 leaves, thin them down to 1 plant every 2 feet. Keep weeds and insects under control.

Although the pumpkin vine will produce many flowers throughout its life, a good rule of thumb is that only 2 pumpkins per vine are typical. Some pumpkins will wither and die soon after flowering. There are several reasons for this. It might be nature's way of letting some die so that good healthy pumpkins live. Another reason for their dying could be perhaps the pumpkins are overcrowded or maybe the weather was too cool, too wet or too dry. Sometimes, it's just difficult to determine.

The size of the pumpkin does depend on variety, but there are other factors that will determine plant growth. Can you think of any? Hmmm. What about the type of soil in the pumpkin patch? We already mentioned water, temperature and number of pumpkins. What else?

The cucumber beetle is a terrible pumpkin pest. It carries plant diseases that can lead to Powdery Mildew. These are bacteria that thrive in hot, humid weather. Just when the pumpkins are getting really big, the bacteria spread and quickly destroy the plant. Keeping the moisture off the leaves will help prevent a bacteria takeover. Watering the patch only in the morning or during the day with soaker hoses will allow the plant to stay dry making a poor environment for the disease. If any plants do become infected, they should be removed and not used in a compost pile. The bacteria can survive and will infect the next year's crop.

If all goes well, by late August, the green pumpkins begin to change color. There will be fewer flowers on the vines because all the plant's energy is directed into the pumpkin. Once the pumpkins have a rich autumn color, it's time for harvest. Leave several inches of the stem to help the melon stay fresh. Protect them from the frost and store in a dry, cool place and they will stay delicious all the way until spring.

? ? ? ? ? ? ? ? ? ? ? ? ? ?

Did you know?
Pumpkins are 90% water.

? ? ? ? ? ? ? ? ? ? ? ? ? ?

Pumpkins come in a variety of colors. Some are white (Lumina), some are blue/green (Australian), and some are deep red-orange (Cinderella). There are giant-sized (Atlantic Giant) pumpkins and wee-bity (Munchkin) pumpkins. There are Buckskin pumpkins, Jack pumpkins, and Baby Boo pumpkins. There are pumpkins with smooth skin and there are pumpkins with warty skin. There is even a pumpkin called a Pie Pumpkin. And do you know why? Because it is just big enough to make one pumpkin pie, that's why.

Besides pumpkin pie, what other foods can you make with pumpkin?

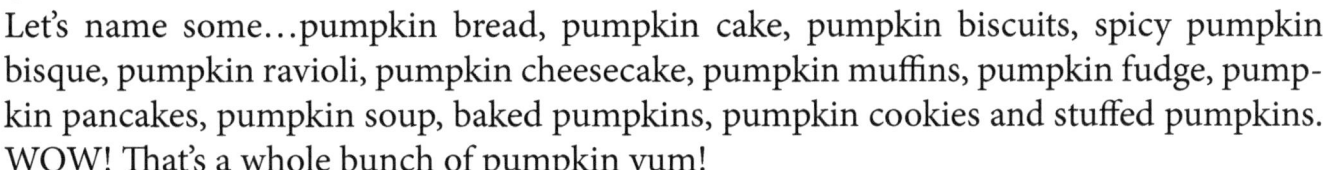

Let's name some…pumpkin bread, pumpkin cake, pumpkin biscuits, spicy pumpkin bisque, pumpkin ravioli, pumpkin cheesecake, pumpkin muffins, pumpkin fudge, pumpkin pancakes, pumpkin soup, baked pumpkins, pumpkin cookies and stuffed pumpkins. WOW! That's a whole bunch of pumpkin yum!

THE LAND

Back in the pioneer days, when folks were migrating from the east coast to go west, they had to cross the plains. The land in the center of the United States wasn't barren, desolate land. It was rich with life.

PRAIRIE GRASS

Many, many years ago, grassland dominated the central one-third of the United States. Among the tall grasses of the prairie three types were prominent: Big bluestem, Indian grass and prairie cord grass. The fine serrated (jagged edges like a sharp steak knife) leaves of prairie cord grass earned it the nickname "rip gut." The tallgrass prairie was so named because the grasses easily grew to 9 feet tall. But, there were more types of grasses than just these three. There were over 150 different kinds of grasses found in the prairie including: little bluestem, prairie dropseed, porcupine grass, sideoats grama and needlegrass. Can you imagine being a pioneer and walking through grasses taller than you with names like rip gut, porcupine and needlegrass? Yikes!

The land was able to support a variety of grasses, but trees were practically nonexistent. Still, the prairie was home to abundant wildlife. What creatures do you think live in the tall grasses of the prairie? If you are very quiet and listen, you might be able to hear some of the animals. Can you hear crickets? Look closely and you might see something other than grass. Do you see any bees or grasshoppers?

The prairie is home to many different kinds of birds, mammals, reptiles, amphibians and, of course, insects. You might be able to see a Ferrungious Hawk or a Western Meadowlark. You may have guessed that Bison, Coyotes, Badgers and Red Fox live hidden in the grass. You would have been correct. But what do those animals eat? How about Black-footed Ferrets and Eastern Cottontail rabbits? Snakes, toads, frogs and lizards also make their home on the prairie. You can find numerous beetles, bees and butterflies going about their business.

When the first settlers moved westward from the forests of the eastern United States, they came upon the prairie, which would have appeared to be an ocean of grass. When the wind would blow across the land, the tall grass would sway in the breeze and appear like ocean waves. In the song America the Beautiful by Katharine Lee Bates, the prairie is described as "O beautiful for spacious skies, for amber waves of grain." Because it looked like an ocean, the first wagons were called prairies schooners.

Pioneers soon discovered that it was easy to become lost in the tall grass because there were no natural landmarks. Just grass as far as the eye could see.

One of the biggest dangers on the prairie is fire. When the wind blows, the flames can travel faster than a person can run. Early settlers plowed up the grass at least 100 yards from their homes and barns to help stop the fires. Flying sparks had to be dashed out with buckets of water and wet gunny sacks.

The prairie is an important habitat for many creatures and part of our nation's history. Folks now do their best to preserve the grassland. Mowing or shredding of the grass is generally done in late fall to eliminate dead material, but letting it stand provides shelter to wildlife throughout the winter. Spring burning rids the grass of weeds, small trees and cool-season grasses. The fire stimulates the growing natural grass. Burning in early spring avoids damaging the grass and wildflower seedlings.

????????????????

Did you know?

Today, native tall grass prairie is the most endangered ecosystem in all of North America.

????????????????

HONEY BEE (*Apis mellifera*)

Female Bee: Queen
Male Bee: Drone
Baby Bee: Larva
Group: Grist, Hive, Swarm
Sound: Hum, Buzz

Many fruits, vegetables, and grasses wouldn't be possible without an insect. One in every three bites of food comes as a direct result of the pollination performed by the honey bee. It is an extremely important insect to farmers and to all of us.

Bees eat honey. While foraging on flowers, worker bees collect nectar by drinking it and storing it in their crop, which is a pouch-like structure similar to a stomach. In addition to nectar, the worker bees store the pollen which has stuck to their body hairs while foraging. A special area on their legs called pollen baskets is where they store the pollen. When they return to the hive, the nectar is regurgitated and given to "house bees". House bees combine the nectar with enzymes and deposit the mixture into a cell (one of the six-sided circle-like structures in the honeycomb). The water in the mixture eventually evaporates leaving behind honey. Pollen is provided to the larvae as a source of protein to ensure healthy development.

Honey bees fly at approximately 15 miles per hour. They will travel up to 9 miles from their hive in order to find food. Typically, when foraging among flowers, bees usually stay within 2 miles of home.

The bees that you will see flying about searching for flowers and nectar are all female. The male bees (drones) don't do any work. They just hang out in the hive (the bees' home). The drones have larger eyes than the worker bees. They look almost as if they have on over-sized sunglasses.

Typically, worker bees live only about 30–35 days. A drone lives approximately 90 days. The queen lives much longer, usually around 3-4 years or even longer.

As worker bees age, their job within the hive changes. For the first 2 days, she acts as a janitor, cleaning cells. From day 3-5, she feeds older larvae and from day 6-11, she feeds younger larvae. She begins to produce wax, build comb and transport food within the hive from days 12-17. From day 18-21, she becomes a guard and protects the entrance to the hive. Not until day 21 does she leave the hive to forage for nectar, pollen and water.

Drones are the male bees and have only one purpose, to mate with the virgin queen. They fly from hive to hive looking for queen bees. Once the queen has mated with several drones, she is able to lay eggs for the rest of her life and will never mate again. When temperatures drop in the autumn, worker bees begin to kill the drones because they no longer have a purpose to the hive and stored honey is too valuable to waste on them. Looking handsome with their "sunglasses" doesn't guarantee them a home for the winter.

The average hive is home to 40,000 – 60,000 bees during late spring and early summer. Farm kept hives may have as many as 80,000 bees!

A honey bee's bright yellow and black pattern is a natural warning sign to potential predators or honey thieves. They do have a weapon that they will use in order to defend the hive. When the hive is threatened, the bees will swarm and attack with their stingers to drive away the intruder. The stinger is a modified egg-laying tube called an ovipositor and a venom gland. Because this is a female structure, only female bees (workers) are able to sting. The stinger has a barb on the end and can only be used once. It rips out of the honey bee's abdomen after use, which kills the bee.

After breeding, a queen begins to lay eggs. She will lay between 1,000-3,000 eggs every day of her 3 to 4 year lifespan! There is only one queen per hive and she is the only bee who lays eggs. A queen is imperative to the health of the hive. Without a living queen, a hive will die within one month. She is so important to the hive that attendant worker bees constantly feed and groom her. Worker bees can cause an egg less than 3 days old to become a queen by feeding her large amounts of royal jelly, which is secreted from glands on the nurse bees' heads.

Beekeepers are also called honey farmers or apiarists and they use bees for honey, wax and pollen. Honey bees are the only insects that produce a food consumed by humans. Honey not only is used as a sweetener, but also as an antimicrobial agent and antioxidant. It has been used for thousands of years as a topical ointment preventing infection. Honey has also been used as a preservative and ancient people used it to prepare bodies for burial.

Bees produce wax. A honey bee must eat about 17-20 pounds of honey to make one pound of bees wax. The main structure of the bee hive is the honeycomb, which is made of beeswax. The honeycomb is made of flat vertical panels of six-sided cells. The bees carefully shape and size the cells for either honey and pollen storage or nursery rooms.

Pollen contains vitamins and amino acids.

? ? ? ? ? ? ? ? ? ? ? ? ? ?

Did you know?
If stored properly, honey will never spoil and will last forever. Yep…it's true!

? ? ? ? ? ? ? ? ? ? ? ? ? ?

CHICKEN (*Gallus domesticus*)

Female Chicken: Hen	**Male Chicken:** Rooster
Young Female Chicken: Pullet	**Young Male Chicken:** Cockerel
	Neutered Male: Capon
Baby Chicken: Chick	**Group:** Flock
	Group of Hens: Brood
Sound: Cluck	**Group of Chicks:** Clutch
Sound of a Rooster: Crow	

Domesticated birds like chickens, turkeys, geese and ducks are called poultry. Farmers raise them for the use of their eggs, feathers and meat.

When you think of a farm and barnyard animal, what animal comes to mind? Do you know the story of Chicken Little? The little fellow thought the sky was falling, but it really wasn't. Perhaps you have heard of The Little Red Hen. She simply wanted to have some bread to eat. Either way, a barnyard wouldn't be complete without a chicken scratching about.

Chickens eat grass, insects, worms, grain, oats, and corn. Chickens also eat apples, grapes, lettuce, peanut butter and jelly sandwiches. They eat crackers, ham and cheese sandwiches, and even pasta. Basically, a chicken will eat anything, including buffalo wings and eggs. Grass is a favorite and the more they eat, the more orange the yolk of their eggs will be. A plus to having chickens on the farm is that they do eat weeds and pesky insects like grasshoppers and crickets.

Typically, a chicken lives 8-10 years. On rare occasions, a chicken can live to be 15 years or older. A chick matures around 6-7 weeks.

A hen will begin laying eggs when she is approximately 4-5 months old. She doesn't need a rooster around to lay eggs, she does this naturally. A rooster is needed to fertilize the eggs to ensure a clutch of chicks. A hen will lay a series of eggs, no more than one or two a day, until she has between 10-12 eggs. Then, she will stop laying and begin brooding, that is sitting on her nest incubating the eggs. It takes 21 days before the eggs begin to hatch. After hatching begins, the hen will remain on her nest for up to 48 hours. Then she will lead her chicks on their first walk. Any eggs not hatched by then will be left behind.

When a farmer collects the eggs, it interrupts the cycle and the hen continues to lay eggs believing she doesn't have enough to start brooding. A hen can lay between 200-300 eggs per year. Roosters are only needed if the farmer wants the eggs fertilized in order to produce chicks.

As hens get older, they don't produce as many eggs. Every now and then, a hen will lay an egg that has no shell. It stays whole, but just doesn't have a shell. Amazing!

If a farmer collects the eggs for market, he'll need to replenish his flocks with new chickens. If he collects the eggs, they won't hatch. Where might the farmer get chicks?

Believe it or not, sometimes farmers mail order their chicks. After the mailman delivers the box of chicks, the farmer carefully places them into a brooder box. This box is specially designed to keep the chicks safe from predators and to keep them warm. Usually, warmth is provided by light bulbs.

The farmer must teach the chicks where to get food and water. This is done by simply dipping the chicks' beaks into the water dish and then into the food dish.

Roosters do serve a purpose beyond just being a dad. Their job on the farm is to crow. They crow whenever they feel like it, not just at sunrise. They crow throughout the day and sometimes during the night. Perhaps they crow to make certain all the other barnyard animals know that the hens are theirs. Perhaps they crow in response to hens clucking. Perhaps they crow just because they like to hear their own voices. They may also crow while performing another duty, that of protecting the flock. That's the real job of the rooster. He is there to keep the social structure of the henhouse secure. One rooster is enough to service 8 to 12 hens. Larger flocks will need more roosters. The rooster tends to stress if forced to be responsible for more than a dozen hens.

Chickens do not like to sleep on the ground. Because they are a prey animal, an animal which is hunted and eaten by other animals, chickens prefer to sleep on a perch.

The hens also prefer to lay eggs in a safe place. Hen boxes are provided for them. A good rule of thumb is one box for every four hens and one to two feet off the ground.

Farmers use chickens for meat and eggs. A chicken weighs between 4-7 pounds. Actual size depends on gender and breed. Roosters weigh more than hens and smaller breeds weigh as little as 1-2 pounds.

Eggs come in a variety of colors, not just white. Some hens lay dark brown eggs, some lay light brown eggs, and some even lay green or blue eggs. The color of the shell has no effect on the nutrients contained in the egg. A good rule of thumb is that the more orange the egg yolk, the healthier and better-tasting the egg will be. Eggs from hens who roam freely are higher in Omega-3 fatty acids and lower in cholesterol than hens kept in cages. To determine what color egg a hen will lay, look at her ear feathers. A hen with white feathers will lay white eggs, but hens with red feathers can lay brown, blue or green eggs. Araucana hens (also known as an Easter Egg Chicken) lay eggs in varying shades of green and blue.

How about chicken nuggets for dinner? Yummy!

TURKEY (*Meleagris gallopava*)

Female Turkey: Hen
Male Turkey: Tom or Gobbler
Young Male Turkey: Jake
Neutered Male: Hokey
Baby Turkey: Poult
Group: Rafter

Sound of a Tom: Gobble
Sound of a Hen: Cluck

Turkeys eat grain, corn, grass and especially love oatmeal. They also eat fruits such as grapes, apples and assorted berries including poison ivy berries. They eat a variety of vegetables, leaves and weeds. Their diet isn't limited to a vegetarian menu as turkeys will eat insects such as beetles and crickets. They also eat mealworms, earthworms, spiders and small animals. They particularly like eating broken chicken eggs. Because turkeys do not have teeth, they need to swallow small rocks or grit (dirt, sand, eggs shells or oyster shells) to have in their gizzards to help grind up their food.

Typically, a wild tom turkey lives 2 years and a wild hen turkey for 3 years. The record life span for a turkey living in captivity is 12 years and 4 months. Domestic turkeys generally do not live longer than one year as they have been breed to grow too heavy to carry their own weight, which for a domestic tom turkey is 50 to 86 pounds. Domestic turkeys are killed for their meat when they are one year old.

After breeding, a hen turkey will lay 8-16 eggs during the nesting period which is from mid-April to mid-June. The eggs will incubate for 28 days before they hatch. Prior to breeding, the tom turkey will fan his tail feathers, fluff his body feathers and strut about while gobbling and grunting. This dance is in attempt to impress the hen turkeys. Unfortunately for domestic tom turkeys, they are too large to breed by themselves and need the farmer's help through artificial insemination. Wild tom turkeys will breed with several hens.

Farmers use turkeys for their meat. In the United States, the average person will eat 15 pounds of turkey a year. Their feathers are also used to make feather dusters. Turkey manure is often used as fertilizer and can be used as a source for energy through a process called gasification.

The turkey originated in North America. The Aztecs domesticated the bird around 500 years ago. After Christopher Columbus voyaged to the continent, the turkey was taken back to Spain. In the early 1500's, the turkey became well-known across Europe. The Pilgrims traveled to New England, bringing the turkey back with them. These turkeys were bred with wild turkeys and the offspring were taken back to England. A man named John Bull selected the birds with the largest breasts and began breeding for that quality. When he traveled to Canada, he brought his "broad-breasted" turkeys with him. Today, the Broad-Breast Bronze turkey is bred only at a handful of hatcheries in the United States.

Domestic turkeys are much larger than their wild cousins. Most are so large that they are too heavy to fly. Wild turkeys fly very well. Because the large domestic turkeys don't fly, they have to be kept safe from predators and are kept in pens. They also need to have shelter. Hay is a good ground cover, but they need a dry place to protect them from rain, wind, hail, sleet and snow. Like chickens, turkeys prefer to sleep off the ground and will roost on perches. The most dominant turkey in the rafter will roost on the highest perch.

Tom turkeys have specialized feathers on their chests that look like long black hair. These feathers are called the beard. They also have fleshy skin dangling under their chins. That skin is called the wattle and the wart-like bumps on his head and neck are called caruncles. Additionally, toms have a bit of skin on top of his beak that can droop down and sag. That is called his snood. When a tom turkey tries to get the attention of a hen turkey, his head becomes bright blue and his snood and wattle get bright red. He fluffs up his feathers to look as big as he can. Hen turkeys seem to enjoy his display.

Turkeys are social animals. It is said that they also enjoy having their feathers stroked. They will even sing along to music.

There are eight types of turkeys recognized by The American Poultry Association. They are Bronze, Narragansett, Bourbon Red, Black, Slate, Royal Palm, Beltsville Small White and the White Holland. The most commonly raised turkey is the White Holland.

? ? ? ? ? ? ? ? ? ? ? ? ? ?

Did you know?
Benjamin Franklin once said the turkey is a "true original native of America." He called the turkey a bird of courage. As a turkey is quick to defend itself and fight against predators, Ben Franklin wanted it, rather than the bald eagle, to be the symbol of the United States.

? ? ? ? ? ? ? ? ? ? ? ? ? ?

GOOSE (*Anser cygnoides*)

Female Goose: Goose	**Male Goose:** Gander
Baby Goose: Gosling	**Group:** Flock, Gaggle, Skein (in flight) Wedge (flying V formation)
Sound of a Tom: Cackle	

Geese eat grass, clover, and corn. Geese are excellent foragers and are content with browsing a pasture and nibbling on lawn clippings. There are choosey eaters and prefer bluegrass, orchard grass, timothy and brome grass. They tend to ignore alfalfa. Goslings may need to be supplemented with corn or pea silage. Geese are excellent for eliminating weeds from cotton and strawberry crops. Geese are not limited to a vegetarian diet. They will eat slugs, snails, frogs, worms, mice and baby rats.

If kept in a pasture, one acre is plenty enough to support 20 to 40 birds

Geese need an ample amount of water. Water troughs need to be deep and wide enough to allow the birds to dip both their bills and their heads. They also need shade to help keep them cool on hot summer days.

Typically, geese can live up to 20 years. Farm geese however, are

sent to market when they weigh 11-15 pounds. Depending on breed and whether or not they've been fed for rapid growth, they may be as young as 10-13 weeks old or 5-6 months old.

Geese are able to reproduce between ages 2 and 3 and will continue to lay eggs until they are approximately 17 years old. They mate for life and will return to the same nesting area year after year. Geese usually build nests in an area near water. Nests are lined with dry grasses, mosses and feathers. They breed just once a year, during March and April. After breeding, a goose will produce a clutch of 2-8 eggs. The eggs are creamy white and will hatch in 25-28 days. Geese will aggressively defend their nests and will harm people if provoked. Should a goose loose her eggs to predators, she will lay a new clutch. The goslings are able to swim and feed within 24 hours of hatching. They fledge (capable of flying) in 6-7 weeks.

Telling a goose from a gander is difficult. Some say that a gander will have blue eyes and a goose will have brown eyes. Some also say that the gander has a shrill, high pitched sound compared to the lower, deeper note of the goose. Unfortunately, neither way is foolproof. Only the geese can tell for sure.

Farmers use geese primarily for meat, especially the liver, and feathers. For centuries, roast goose, succulent in texture and full of flavor, has been the food of choice for royalty and dignitaries. It makes an excellent meal to celebrate festive occasions. Even Ebenezer Scrooge wanted goose for Christmas dinner. The French have specialized in transforming fresh goose liver into a variety of pates and special dishes. The soft feathers of geese, called down, are used for stuffing quality pillows and assorted bedding.

Geese will lose their flight feathers once a year usually in July. This is called "molting." It is during this time that they are easily captured. Geese should never be chased. They walk slowly and get stressed. It is easy to herd them into holding pens. A long wire crook can be used to catch the goose by the neck. Another way is to use a fisherman's net. A goose should never be caught by the legs as this could cause injury. When handling a goose, it is important to be careful. They can bite and scratch. They also can use their wings to inflict painful blows. This is called flogging. If you have ever been bitten or flogged by a goose, you will always remember the experience!

In addition to being used for meat and feathers, geese do provide another service to the farm. Geese are loud. They hiss and honk at anyone coming too close. This behavior makes them excellent barnyard "watch dogs." It is extremely difficult to sneak up on a goose.

? ? ? ? ? ? ? ? ? ? ? ? ?

Did you know?

One is a goose. Two or more are geese. There is no such thing as gooses.

? ? ? ? ? ? ? ? ? ? ? ? ?

Different Types of Geese

The Toulouse is a grey goose weighing up to 30 pounds. They have a soft appearance and are rarely aggressive.

The Chinese goose is a lightly built goose and has an upright posture. They come in a brown and a white variety. The Chinese gander is taller than the goose and has a large round knob above his bill. Chinese geese make great watchdogs as they are high spirited honkers.

The African goose is a breed that is a cross between a Toulouse and a brown Chinese. It weighs up to 26 pounds. They are bold, vocal birds that can carry themselves upright to a height of 3 feet. They are ashy brown, edged with a lighter shade of brown. Hand reared, they make wonderful pets.

The Embden goose is the tallest of the breeds reaching up to just over 3 feet. Its plumage is pure white. They have long graceful necks, short tails and blue eyes.

DUCK (*Anas domesticus*)

Female Duck: Duck

Baby Duck: Duckling

Sound: Quack

Male Duck: Drake

Group: Brace, Bunch, Flock, Paddle, Raft, or Team

Ducks eat grass, insects, worms, slugs, corn, snails, crabs, shrimp, barnacles, tadpoles and frogs. It really depends on the type of duck. Mallard ducks (the males have green heads) eat seeds, mosquito larvae and mayfly nymphs. Merganser ducks (these are larger ducks with brown heads, white bodies and thin bills) prefer minnows, trout and some amphibians. Domestic ducks have been known to eat mice and even spaghetti!

?? ? ? ?? ? ?? ? ?? ? ?

Did you know?

Bread is bad for ducks. It makes them feel "full" and then they don't eat healthy natural items critical for their nutrition and survival. Overfed or malnourished ducks are sluggish and can't escape from predators.

?? ? ? ?? ? ?? ? ?? ? ?

Typically, a domestic duck lives 10-15 years. Wild ducks can live up to 20 years, but the oldest living duck was a Mallard drake that lived for 27 years! Unfortunately, domestic ducks released into the wild aren't so lucky. Those ducks only live around 3 years.

When most people imagine what a duck looks like, they think of the Pekin Duck. It is a white duck with an orange bill, legs and feet. The Pekin ducklings are bright yellow and are commonly seen around Easter. It is the typical domestic duck. It has an even temperament and makes a good pet. The most famous Pekin Duck is…Donald Duck!

Pekin drakes and ducks are both white. How can you tell which one is which? Easy! Just look at their tail feathers. Drakes will have two or three curly feathers on the top of their tails.

A duck will lay approximately 9-11 eggs.

Winter is when ducks usually look for a mate. The drakes, with their colorful plumage will attract female ducks. The Mallard duck is a good example of how much more colorful males are than females. Drake Mallard ducks have bright green heads while female Mallard ducks are brown. Once the female duck has selected a drake, come spring, she will lead him to the breeding ground, very near where she was hatched. She will build a nest using grass or reeds. Sometimes she will use a hole in a tree. It's the drake who guards their territory by chasing away other pairs.

The female duck lays her eggs, which will take 28 days to hatch and they will hatch within 24 hours of each other. Muscovy ducks (large ducks with fleshy faces) usually lay 12-15 eggs. The ducklings are precocial, which means they are able to swim and feed themselves immediately after hatching. The mother duck will protect her brood from predators like raccoons, turtles and snakes until they are old enough to fly, which is around 5-8 weeks.

A Pekin duck mother is an amazing egg layer. She will lay up to 200 eggs a season! Unfortunately, she doesn't tend to her eggs very well. If the farmer wants to have ducklings, he will need to take the eggs to an incubator in order for them to hatch.

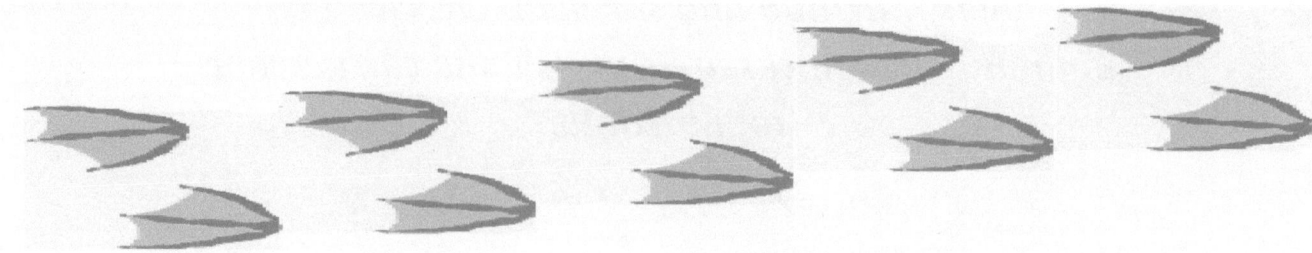

Farmers use ducks for eggs, meat and feathers (down). The Eider duck (a large sea duck) plucks down from her breast to line her nest and cover her eggs. Once she and the ducklings have abandoned the nest, the eiderdown is gathered by the farmer. These feathers are used as stuffing for quilts and pillows. Eiderdown is extremely rare, and is the softest, lightest and warmest down in the world.

But what about their feet? There are no feathers on their feet. The duck has special blood vessels inside his feet called capillaries. When their feet start to get cold, the capillaries constrict forcing the blood into bigger blood vessels called arteries. The blood in the arteries is warm and heat is exchanged to the colder blood. The whole process keeps the duck's feet warm. Pretty neat, huh?

? ? ? ? ? ? ? ? ? ? ? ? ? ?

Did you know?

A duck's feathers are waterproof? Yep, it's true. This adaptation helps the ducks stay warm even in the coldest winter months. The feathers prevent the cold water from actually touching the duck's body.

? ? ? ? ? ? ? ? ? ? ? ? ? ?

GOAT (*Capra hircus*)

Female Dairy Goat: Doe
Female Meat Goat: Nanny

Baby Goat: Kid

Sound: Bleat

Male Dairy Goat: Buck
Male Meat Goat: Billy
Nuetered Male: Wether
Group: Tribe, Trip, Drove

Livestock are domesticated animals raised in an agricultural setting to produce commodities such as food, fiber and labor.

Goats eat grass, hay, grain, oats, corn, and alfalfa. Although many cartoons depict goats eating tin cans, they in fact do not. Goats are curious animals and will sniff and nibble new things, especially shirt tails, rubber boots and hats. They will, however, eat peanut butter and jelly sandwiches, carrots and grapes. A benefit to having goats is that they also eat weeds and other vegetation that cows and horses ignore. Goats will eat thistle and poison ivy. Drinking milk from a goat that has consistently eaten poison ivy is thought to build up immunity against the ill effects of poison ivy.

Goats are curious animals and have very sensitive lips. They explore their environment by tasting, mouthing or smelling potential food. They are only interested in food that is clean and tasty. Soiled or spoiled food will be ignored.

If a goat were to smile, you would notice that they don't have any top teeth. Where the top teeth should be, there is a hard pad. Food is pressed against this pad and snipped off by the lower teeth. The 24 molars in the back of the mouth, both on the top and the bottom, grind up the food for easy swallowing.

Goats belong to a group of animals called ruminants. This group of animals "chews their cud." Basically, grass and vegetation is difficult to digest so they have to eat it twice. The first time the food is swallowed it enters into the first of four chambers of the stomach, the rumen. The rumen stores the food in a soup of bacteria and other micro-organisms that help break it down. When it is thoroughly soaked with digestive enzymes and saliva, the goat regurgitates (vomits) back into its mouth and chews the food (cud) for a second time! Isn't that amazing? If you closely watch a goat's neck you can see food go down and back up. Rumination builds up excess gas in the stomach so goats have to burp to prevent themselves from swelling.

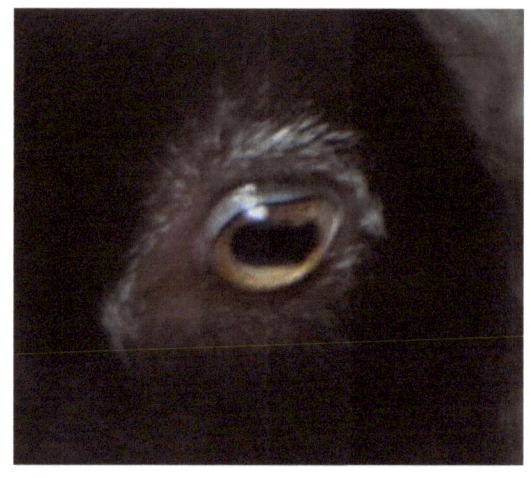

A goat's eye is special, too. The pupils aren't round like mine and yours. Their pupils are rectangular in shape. It is believed that this characteristic allows them to see well in the dark. Excellent night vision enables them to graze long after the sun has set. Most goats have yellow or brown eyes. Blue eyes are rare.

Typically, a doe can live about 12 years, a buck about 10 years and wethers can live up to 16 years.
After breeding, a doe or nanny will give birth in five months or approximately 150 days. Typically, goats produce twins, but singles and triplets are not uncommon. Goats are lively and social animals. They love to climb (especially Alpine goats), run and jump. Some breeds of goats can jump well over 5 feet! They are agile animals that can crawl under fences and stand on their hind legs. Goats are quite intelligent and easily learn to open latches on farm gates.

Goats prefer to stay in groups of their own kind. In a mixed breed herd, goats will separate themselves into like breed groups. Kids prefer to remain near their mother, even after they have grown up.

Farmers use goats primarily for milk, cheese and meat. Dairy goats provide milk that is used for human consumption. More people in the world drink goat's milk than cow's milk. Goat's milk is similar in nutritional value to cow's milk, but it has smaller fat globules and therefore is easier for some people to digest. It also does not require homogenization. Additionally, goat's milk is lower in cholesterol and higher in calcium, iron, phosphorus and vitamins A and B than cow's milk.

Goat's milk can be used in a number of ways. Not only is it good to drink, the milk can be used for cooking and baking. Butter can be made after separating the cream. Many types of cheeses can be made from goat's milk. A soft goat cheese, called chevre, can be substituted in any recipe calling for cream cheese. Mozzarella and ricotta cheese can also be made with goat's milk, as well as yogurt and ice cream. Additionally, goat's milk is used to make creamy and natural soap.

??????????????

Did you know?

Nearly 63% of red meat consumed world-wide is goat meat? Chevon (meat from an adult goat) or cabrito (meat from a young goat) is low in fat and a good tasting alternative to chicken or fish. Additionally, the texture of goat meat differs from other meats and is more easily digested. The taste is a mild veal-like flavor.

?????????????

Different Types of Goats

Nubian goats, have long, floppy ears. They are a larger breed of goat and can produce an average of 3 quarts (6 pounds) of milk each day, but some have been known to give up to 1 ½ gallons.

La Mancha goats are unique in that they have very tiny ears. They are calm and gentle. They have a straight nose and are a small breed.

Alpine goats are a medium-large breed and have erect ears. They can be any color except solid white and light brown with white markings. Like Nubian goats, Alpine goats are a popular dairy breed because they can produce a significant amount of milk.

Boer goats are the most popular breed in the world to be used for meat.

COW (*Bos taurus*)

Female Cow: Cow
Female Young Cow: Heifer
Baby Cow: Calf

Sound: Moo
Sound by Bull: Bellow

Male Cow: Bull
Nuetered Male: Steer
Group: Herd, Drove, Kine, Drift, Mob

Cows eat grass, hay, corn, oats and alfalfa. They also eat soybeans, cottonseed, peanut meal, almond hulls, chicken feathers, fish and pumpkins. They use their tongues to pull grass; grazing up to 8 hours a day consuming over 100 pounds of food. Cows need to drink 25 to 50 gallons of water a day. That is nearly a bathtub full!

> ❓❓❓❓❓❓❓❓❓❓❓❓
>
> ***Did you know?***
> *Dairy cows can produce up to 200 pounds of flatus (farts and burps) a day!*
>
> ❓❓❓❓❓❓❓❓❓❓❓❓

To make 1 gallon of milk, a cow must drink 2 gallons of water.

Cows, like goats, belong to a group of animals called ruminants. When they swallow their food, it enters into the first of 4 chambers of the stomach called the rumen. The rumen can hold up to 50 gallons of food. Wow, that's a whole bunch! The rumen stores the food and mixes it with digestive enzymes and bacteria. After a thorough soaking, the cow regurgitates (ruminates) back into its mouth to chew it for a second time. They will spend 8 hours a day chewing their cud (regurgitated food).

Also like goats, cows do not have any top teeth in the front of their mouths. They grab their food with their tongues. They first stick out their tongue, wrap it around the food and then pull it all back inside where the molars (back teeth) grind it. The tongue is used for another purpose, too. Can you think of what that might be? Well, cows don't come with tissue, so when they get runny noses, cows will stick their tongues in their noses and lick out the juices. Ewww!

Typically, a cow lives about 25 years. The oldest cow on record was Big Bertha who died 3 months shy of her 49th birthday. During her lifetime, a cow spends 13 hours a day lying down and gets up an average of 14 times. Each day, she produces 65 pounds of poop!

A cow will breed when she is about 2 years old and will give birth, usually to a single calf in nine months. A newborn calf weighs between 80-100 pounds. The largest calf born weighed 225 pounds! That's a BIG baby! Typically, there is one bull for every 30 cows in a herd. He is the daddy of all the babies.

Cows have cloven hooves. Their feet actually help them to not get stuck in the mud. Their toes spread, making their feet wider so they don't sink as deep as animals with a solid hoof, like a horse. The space between their toes prevents a vacuum when they pull their

feet out of the mud making it easier to free themselves. This means a cow can outrun a horse if they were to race in deep mud.

Farmers use cows primarily for milk and meat. Dairy cows, those used for milk, can give over 6 gallons of milk each day. A healthy cow gives about 200,000 glasses of milk in her lifetime. What a cow eats affects how much milk she makes and how it tastes. A cow that eats only grass can give about 50 glasses of milk a day. A cow that eats grass, corn, hay and mixed feeds can produce about 100 glasses of milk a day.

Milk is used to make butter, cream, yogurt, whipped cream, cottage cheese and cheese. It takes 12 pounds (5.6 quarts) of milk to make 1 gallon of ice cream. It takes 10 pounds (4.6 quarts) of milk to make 1 pound of cheese.

Today's cows can produce much more milk than they could many years ago. Before the milking machine was invented in 1894, farmers had to milk by hand. It takes 350 squirts to fill a gallon of milk. It took an hour to milk 6 cows. With machines, farmers can milk more than 100 cows in an hour.

Beef cows, those used for meat, provide not only food, but also a variety of other products. Industrial cleaners, fertilizer, pot cleaners, brass and tooth polish. Glue made from cow's blood is used to make plywood. The horns and hooves provide the proteins that make foam for fire extinguishers. Stearic acid makes rubber hold its shape and used in automobile and bicycle tires. Gelatin is used in pie crust, jelly beans, marshmallows and photographic film. One cow hide can make 144 baseballs or 20 footballs or 18 soccer balls or 12 basketballs.

Different Types of Cows

Holstein cows are the black and white spotty cows. Their spots are like fingerprints; no two cows have the same pattern. They are larger than Jersey cows and give more milk.

Jersey cows are brown cows. They give less milk than Holsteins, but more cream.

Herford cows are large red cows used for beef.

Angus cows are large black cows used for beef.

If you wanted to eat steak with your mashed potatoes and gravy, what animal would you need?

SHEEP (*Ovis aries*)

Female Sheep: Ewe

Baby Sheep: Kid

Sound: Bleat, Baa

Male Sheep: Ram
Nuetered Male: Wether
Group: Drove, Flock

Sheep eat grass, hay, clover, weeds, and grain. When sheep are allowed to forage in a pasture, they will eat the weeds first and prefer the young and tender shoots. Pregnant ewes or ewes with lambs and growing lambs require additional nutrients and are feed grains such as corn, wheat, barley and oats. Because they love to eat grain, they will over eat and make themselves sick. Shepherds (those who tend sheep) must take caution to not over feed their sheep. When allowed to graze in a pasture, sheep will spend up to seven hours a day eating.

Like a goat and a cow, sheep are ruminants. (Do you remember what ruminant means?) They have split upper lips with which they can readily select their favorite plants.

? ? ? ? ? ? ? ? ? ? ? ? ? ?

Did you know?

One is a sheep. Two or more are sheep. There is no such thing as sheeps.

? ? ? ? ? ? ? ? ? ? ? ? ? ?

Sheep can live between 10 and 20 years. Typically they live 6 to 13 years. The breed, size, nutrition and the farmer's intent determine the lifespan.

Probably the most famous sheep is Dolly. She was the world's first animal to be cloned. Dolly was born in Scotland on July 5, 1995, from three different mothers. One ewe provided the DNA, the second provided the egg into which the DNA was injected and a third ewe carried the embryo and gave birth to Dolly. It took 276 tries to get the process correct and when she was finally born, Dolly was a scientific superstar.

After breeding, a ewe will "lamb" or give birth in five months, or approximately 150 days, but individual pregnancies may vary from 138 to 159 days. Most ewes will be ready for breeding when they are between the ages of 5 and 12 months, with breed, size and nutrition affecting the onset of puberty. A first time mother will generally have a single baby. After that, twins are more common. Some ewes, when between the ages of 3 and 6 years, can give birth to "litters" of lambs consisting of four, five or even six lambs.

Lambs are precocial (independent), meaning they can stand shortly after birth. Sheep are gregarious, social animals and prefer to flock together. It is rare to see one by itself. Remaining in a flock is one way to protect themselves from predators; after all, they are defenseless against coyotes and wild dogs.

Farmers and shepherds use sheep for wool, meat, milk and other products. Like pigs, humans use every part of the sheep. The horns, hooves and bones are rich in keratin and collagen and are used to make products like adhesive tape, marshmallows, piano keys and gelatin desserts like ice cream, yogurt and jello. Instrument strings and suture material are made from the intestines and sheep fat and fatty acids are transformed into a number of items. Included in the assorted list of products are crayons, candles, floor wax, cosmetics, tanning lotion, and shaving cream. Sheep are essential to the great American past-time of baseball. The ball is stuffed with wool and sewn together with wool thread. The rubber lining is made from stearic acid and the cork center contains processed blood. Besides wool socks, mittens, and other clothing, wool is used to make lanolin, artist brushes, insulation and rug pads.

Depending on the size and breed of sheep, one sheep can produce 2 to 30 pounds of wool annually. On average, sheep in the United States produce 8.2 pounds of fleece (wool from one sheep) each year. Wool from white sheep and sheep with white faces is more desirable than dark sheep wool. The darker fibers cannot be dyed, limiting them to their natural color.

After wool is removed from the sheep, the fleece is divided into separate categories based on length and fineness of the fibers. The wool is then washed in hot, soapy water to remove the dirt and a natural grease called lanolin.

The lanolin is collected during the process of cleaning the wool. It is used in a variety of products like adhesive tape, printing ink and motor oil. When refined, lanolin is used in cosmetics and pharmaceuticals. Lipsticks, mascara, lotions, shampoos and hair conditions contain lanolin.

After washing and drying, the wool enters into a carding machine where brushes with fine wire teeth remove any debris like burrs and straw. Then the wool is straightened and combed into a fine layer. Depending on the thickness of the wool fibers, it is separated into a woolen or worsted category.

Woolen yarn is made of shorter and thicker fibers that lie in several directions and is used to make thicker fabrics like tweed.

Worsted yarn is made of long, fine fibers that produce a smoother fabric. About half of the wool products made in the United States use worsted yarn.

The meat obtained from sheep is rich in vitamins and proteins needed for healthy living. Sheep meat is the principle meat eaten in North Africa, the Middle East, India and parts of Europe. Europe is the world's larger consumer of sheep and the number one importer of lamb. Lamb meat is from a sheep less than one year old. Meat from sheep older than a year is called mutton.

Sheep can be used for having fun. A rodeo event called "mutton busting" is for children ages 4 to 7 and under 60 pounds. Wearing helmets for safety, the contestants try to ride a sheep bareback for 6 seconds. Although sheep aren't known to buck, the dash across the arena dislodges most riders.

 If you wanted to play a game of baseball, what two animals would you need?

PIG (*Sus scrofa*)

Female Pig: Sow
Young Female Pig: Gilt
Baby Pig: Piglet

Male Pig: Boar
Nuetered Male Pig: Barrow
Group: Drift, Drove

Sound: Squeal, Grunt

Pigs eat grain, barley, wheat, sorghum, soybean and corn. Pigs will generally eat most anything except for glass and metal. They especially love slops, which is a mixture of all kinds of vegetables and kitchen scraps. Milk and dairy products are favorites and seem to help control internal parasites. Pigs will eat ham and cheese sandwiches. They love eggs and will eat the shells, too.

Pigs are omnivores, meaning they eat plants and animals. Their noses, called snouts, are highly sensitive and they can sniff out all kinds of foods including, insects, worms, tree bark, leaves, roots, fruits, flowers, rotting carcasses and garbage. Nothing seems to stop them from hunting for food. Because of their diet and desire to eat and eat, pigs have been able to survive throughout the world, on every continent except Antarctica.

Typically, a pig lives 10-15 years. The type of pig can affect the average life span. A pig is generally considered to be full grown by three and a half years old, but some pigs keep growing until they are 5 years old.

After breeding, a sow will give birth in just less than four months or approximately 114 days. Labor can last anywhere from 30 minutes to 5 hours with 15 minutes between piglets. A typical litter will be 8 to 12 piglets, but can be many more.

Farmers use pigs primarily for meat. A pig becomes a hog when it weighs 120 pounds. When the hogs are about 6 months old, they weigh around 220-260 pounds and that's when they are sent to market. Humans use pigs for bacon, sausage, pepperoni, hotdogs, ham and other cuts of pork. Have you ever eaten pork rinds or cracklins? How about pulled pork, fatback, lardo, pancetta, guanciale lomo, chipolatas, sausage, bratwurst, ham, pork chops, bacon, boccalone, prosciutto, chitterlings or chitlins, scrapple, bologna, mu shu pork, pork roast, BBQ pork, or sweet and sour pork? Pork is mighty tasty.

Pigs also provide humans with nearly 40 drugs and pharmaceuticals, like insulin. There are approximately 500 by-products made from pigs. Some examples are fertilizer, glass, china, floor wax, chalk, and crayons. Their skin can be tanned to make leather products, like footballs, and because it is similar to human skin it is used in skin grafts for treating burns. Their heart valves are used to replace human heart valves which have been damaged or weakened. Pig hair, called bristles, is used to make paint brushes and gelatin and bubble gum are made from pig fat.

Other products that use the pig are shampoos, toothpaste, shaving cream, matches, buttons and cake frosting. Several dairy products use a pork enzyme called rennet in their processing. Among them are whipped cream, sour cream and cheese.

? ? ? ? ? ? ? ? ? ? ? ? ?

Did you know?

Pigs don't sweat. Yep, it's true. That's why they love to wallow in the mud. The mud helps keep them cool on hot summer days. It also helps protect them from sunburn and from being bitten by insects. When they are bitten by a pesky bug, they will try to scratch. They will rub against fencing, housing, and everything else. They also love to play with toys and each other. A favorite game of pigs is Chase.

? ? ? ? ? ? ? ? ? ? ? ? ?

DONKEY (*Equus asinus*)

Female Donkey: Jennet	**Male Donkey:** Jack
	Nuetered Male Donkey: Gelding
Baby Donkey: Foal	**Group:** Drove , Pace, Herd
Sound: Bray	

Though not raised for food or fiber, the donkey is a valuable animal for labor.

Donkeys eat grass, hay, and grain. Donkeys are suited to grasses not rich in protein. As they are a desert animal, they can gain weight quickly. An overfed donkey will develop a fat pad on the neck and once it's there, it tends to stay. Only on rare occasion, treats such as an animal cracker, ginger snap, graham cracker or other low-fat cookie can be given. Nutritious apples are a good option for a treat. Treats are best kept to a minimum as a donkey will come to expect a treat and can become quite demanding.

Food given to other barnyard animals like cows, pigs and chickens may be harmful for donkeys. Rhododendrons, nightshade, ragwort and yew are just some plants that are extremely dangerous for donkeys. Donkeys should never be given meat products.

Because donkeys love to eat, if a farmer notices a lack of appetite, there is cause for concern.

Typically, a donkey can live to be around 40 years old. Their life span normally falls between 30 to 50 years.

After breeding, a jennet will give birth in 11 months, but a pregnancy can last up to 14 months. Although donkeys generally do not produce twins, it can happen and occurs more frequently in donkeys than in horses.

Donkeys are predominately gray, although they can come in other colors like brown, black, sorrel and white. All donkeys have some form of a cross patter on their backs. The line extends down the length of their backs and across their shoulders. This mark is called the Donkey's Cross. The cross on true black donkeys is not visible. Spotted donkeys can have a dotted line.

Farmers use donkeys for work, companionship, guarding sheep or goats, milk, and halter breaking young horses. Donkeys are commonly used in recreational riding and pulling of carts/wagons. As a pack animal, they can carry equipment on its back and walk alongside the farmer. This practice is convenient as a donkey's walking pace is the same as a human's.

Donkeys make excellent companion animals for young foals, especially at weaning time. The donkey's calming influence reduces stress in the young animal during separation from its mother. Additionally, a donkey will readily approach humans and encourages the foal to develop a friendly attitude toward humans. The tranquil disposition also works to steady nervous horses kept in a stable and relaxes those recovering from an injury or surgery.

Once a donkey has been introduced to a sheep or goat and bonded with that animal, it makes for a superb guard while in the pasture. Donkeys are alert, intelligent and cautious animals and will defend its pasture mates from coyotes and foxes as it would one of its own. If there is a strange sound, the donkey will alert the herd and chase and often trample the predator. Unfortunately, miniature donkeys tend to be too small to protect against coyotes and mammoth donkeys are too slow. A benefit to having a donkey rather than a working dog is that donkeys eat the same food as its grazing companions.

Donkeys are slower and less powerful than horses, but they are extremely intelligent with a strong sense of survival. If they think some activity is dangerous, they just won't do it! Donkeys are definitely patient and persistent.

Donkey's milk may be considered an alternative to powdered milks, soybean milk or other formulas for infant nutrition since its composition in lipids and proteins is very close to human milk.

HORSE (*Equus caballus*)

Female Horse: Mare
Young Female Horse: Filly

Baby Horse: Foal

Sound: Neigh, Whinny

Male Horse: Stallion
Young Male Horse: Colt
Nuetered Male Horse: Gelding
Group: Herd, Stable, Mob

In the United States, horses are raised for labor and companionship. Some people consider them as livestock and some people consider them as pets. In other countries, horses are raised for food.

Horses eat grass, hay, grain, oats, corn, and alfalfa. The best and most natural food for a horse is good quality pasture. They like peas and carrots, too. They especially love treats

like apples, pears and watermelons. Molasses is a big favorite as are peppermint candies. In a pasture of mixed grasses and clover, horses will pick out their favorites. Some horses even enjoy munching on weeds like thistles. Those spikey thorns around the blossoms don't seem to bother horses. They also love dandelions. Young horses can benefit from eating seaweed. Working horses need added protein and can be fed one or two eggs a day.

Depending on the size, breed and work demands of a horse, the amount of food required for a healthy weight is varied. A general rule of thumb is that for every 100 pounds of body weight, a horse will need to eat 2-2.2 pounds of feed. So a horse weighing 1000 pounds will need 20–25 pounds of food, mostly grass. Horses also need to drink between 5-10 gallons of water each day. Salt encourages horses to drink and aids in digestion.

There are many plants that are harmful to horses. Oak trees and acorns, walnut trees and walnuts should not be around pastures. Foxglove, nightshade, rhododendron and poppies may be pretty to look at, but should never be around horses.

? ? ? ? ? ? ? ? ? ? ? ? ? ? ?

Did you know?

Horses produce approximately 10 gallons of saliva a day.

? ? ? ? ? ? ? ? ? ? ? ? ? ? ?

Typically, a horse lives between 20-30 years. The oldest horse on record lived for 62 years.

It is said it is possible to determine a horse's age based upon looking at his teeth. There is some truth to that. Their teeth grow continuously until they are between the ages of 25 and 30. The teeth of young horses are smaller than those of older horses. Unlike cows and goats, horses do have front teeth on top and bottom. They have 12 incisors, 6 on top and 6 on bottom, that are used to snip off vegetation, plus they have molars for grinding their food. Eating natural grasses grinds the teeth down evenly. When grain is added to their diet, sometimes the back molars wear unevenly causing sharp ridges to form. That's when the veterinarian is needed to "float" the teeth. Basically, the vet files them down to make them even again.

Unlike cows and goats, horses do not have 4 chamber stomachs. They have a regular stomach like humans. The stomach leads into the small intestine, which is about 70 feet long and holds up to 12 gallons! This is where the majority of digestion takes place. What

? ? ? ? ? ? ? ? ? ? ? ? ? ?

Did you know?
Horses are able to sleep both standing up and lying down. They sleep in short intervals of about 15 minutes for a total of just a couple of hours each day.

? ? ? ? ? ? ? ? ? ? ? ? ? ?

the body doesn't need, it gets rid of, out the back end. A horse poops about 10 times a day, equaling about 51 pounds! The poop is excellent fertilizer for gardens and farm land. Because horses have eyes on the sides of their heads, they are able to see almost all the way around their bodies. Directly in front of their noses and directly behind their tails are the only places where a horse can't see.

After breeding, a mare will give birth in approximately 11 months or around 343 days. A single foal is the norm, however twins, though extremely rare (about 1 in every 10,000 births) do occur.

Farmers use horses for many purposes. The draft horses (nicknamed "gentle giants") are bred for strength and a calm and patient temperament. They pull plows or heavy wagons full of people. Draft horses stand 16.0 to 18.0 hands high (64-72 inches) and weight 1,500-2,000 pounds. The largest horse in history was named Sampson. He was 21.2 ½ hands high (86.5 inches) and weighed 3,360 pounds. That is more than what a car weighs!

Miniature horses are used for pulling miniature wagons; guide animals for the blind; therapy animals and pets. The earliest history of miniature horses was in 1650 A.D. at the Palace at Versailles in the zoo kept by King Louis XIV. The world's smallest horse, named Thumbelina is only 17 inches tall and weighs 60 pounds.

Horses are also used for their meat either for human consumption or in pet food. The tail hair of horses can be used for making the bows for violins. Some people even drink horse milk.

? ? ? ? ? ? ? ? ? ? ? ? ? ?

Did you know?
If you breed a donkey with a horse, you end up with a mule. Unfortunately, mules cannot have babies.

? ? ? ? ? ? ? ? ? ? ? ? ? ?

BLACK RAT SNAKE
(*Elapha obsolete*)

Female Snake: Snake

Male Snake: Snake

Baby Snake: Snakelet, Neonate, Hatchling

Group: Bed, Nest, Pit

Sound: Hiss

*I*n the barn, the farmer stores feed and grain for his animals. If the farmer grows crops, there will be seeds either in the barn or in the fields. Either way, feed, grain and seeds are delicious food for an unwelcome animal: the mouse.

Farmers do not want to feed rodents. For that reason, he welcomes the barn cat to the farm. There is another animal that is welcome on the farm that eats mice. Can you think what animal that might be?

Although not part of the family and not considered a barnyard animal, the black snake plays a vital part on the farm.

Black Rat Snakes found on the farm eat mice and rats. They will eat birds and birds' eggs and will often raid the hen boxes for an easy meal. For this reason, these snakes have also been called "Chicken Snakes." Black Rat Snakes are excellent climbers and spend a large amount of time in trees. Frogs, especially tree frogs, are on the menu. Squirrels and lizards have been known to end up as a meal. Often, the Black Rat Snake uses the hollows of other mammals and birds.

Typically, a Black Rat Snake will live up to 20 years. As snakes are territorial, it is reasonable to believe that the farmer sees the same snakes year after year around the barn.

In the spring, between March and May, snakes emerge from winter hibernation. By May and early June, they seek out a mate. The male snakes generally wait for a female to pass through his territory. In late summer, about five weeks after breeding, the female will lay a clutch of 12-20 eggs in a well hidden place, under hollow logs or in abandoned burrows. Between 65-70 days after that, the hatchlings emerge hungry. They are vigorous eaters, eating lizards, baby mice, chipmunks, and small frogs, and will quickly double their size. Black Rat Snakes usually will migrate back to their hibernation dens in October.

Black Rat Snakes are large snakes. Adults range from 42-72 inches. Snakes reaching longer than six feet are not rare. Sometimes they can even reach eight feet long.

They are not venomous, but they will bite. They are shy snakes and tend to freeze when first encountering danger. Some adults attempt to protect themselves by coiling their bodies and vibrating their tails. If picked up, they will release a foul-smelling musk and spread it around with their tails.

Black Rat Snakes are shiny black. They have keeled scales (a raised ridge line down the middle of each scale) that make it appear to be rough. There may be small flecks of whitish color on their scales, but their chins and bellies do have white markings. Sometimes, after eating a big meal, it is possible to see white between their scales.

Black Rat Snakes are often confused with Northern Black Racers, Black Kingsnakes, Cornsnakes, Eastern Milksnakes and sometimes Northern Copperheads. Most of the time the species confusion comes from attempts to identify the juvenile snake. Juvenile Black Rat Snakes have a brown banded pattern. When in doubt, simply leave the snake alone. Even though mild-tempered, the Black Rat Snake will bite and thrash if captured.

*If you wanted to have bacon and eggs for breakfast,
what two animals would you need?*

OUTHOUSE

The term outhouse refers to any building away from the main house and used for any purpose not wanted in the house. But in this case, the term outhouse refers to the outside building that houses the toilet.

On the prairie, there were three buildings that held importance to early farmers; the main house, the barn and the outhouse. Due to the odor associated with the outhouse, the structure was generally built between 50 – 150 feet from the main house.

A well-planned farm placed the pathway between the outhouse and the main house along the side of the garden, the woodpile and the well. On a farm, chores are never finished and a trip to the privy meant bringing back vegetables from the garden, wood for the wood box and a pail of water for the kitchen on the return trip.

The average outhouse had no heat, electricity and no window. The crescent-shaped cut-out allowed for ventilation. It also served as a way to distinguish the ladies' outhouse from the gentlemen's outhouse. For those who couldn't read. The outhouse for men was said to have a star-shaped cutout. The men's outhouses typically were unkempt and not well maintained and as a result, the women's outhouse with the crescent moon survived.

Most outhouses contained two holes of different sizes; one for the adults and a smaller one for the children. Larger families had outhouses with several holes to allow for simultaneous use.

When nature called, folks visited the outhouse through the rain, wind, storms, cold, and heat. When winter set in, their visits to the outhouse were an affair for courage, hardiness and real necessity. Jack Frost would nip at a visitor's backside resulting in a hasty scamper back to the kitchen to sit by a warm fire.

Today, toilet paper is routinely used. Please remember to wash your hands after each visit. Soap and water help prevent the spread of disease. and real necessity. Jack Frost would nip at a visitor's backside resulting in a hasty scamper back to the kitchen to sit by a warm fire. Toilet paper was a luxury not easily afforded by farm families. Corn cob wipes were used instead. YOWZERS! To make them softer, the cobs were soaked and then hung or piled in baskets on the floor. The variety of the corn impacted the color of the cobs. Red cobs were frequently used followed by lighter cobs so the user could ensure sufficient wiping. Newspapers and pages from old catalogs were also used in the tidying process.

Today, toilet paper is routinely used. Please remember to wash your hands after each visit. Soap and water help prevent the spread of disease.

GLOSSARY

Amino Acid—the building blocks of protein.

Carcass—the dead body of an animal.

Chitterlings (chitlins)—the small intestine of swine, especially when prepared for food.

Cloven—cleft, split, divided

Domestic—pertaining to the home, tame.

Enzyme—a protein in a living cell that aids in a chemical reaction, like digestion.

Feral—existing in a natural state, not domesticated, wild.

Gizzard—a thick-walled, muscular pouch in the lower stomach of many birds and reptiles that grinds food, often with the aid of ingested stones or grit.

Hatchery—a place for hatching eggs.

Hibernate—to spend the winter in close quarters in a dormant condition, as bears and certain other animals.

Homogenize—by reducing the size of the fat globules in (milk or cream)

Infest—to live in or overrun to an unwanted degree or in a troublesome manner, especially as predatory animals or vermin do.

Kerosene—a type of fuel.

Kindling—material that can be readily ignited, used in starting a fire.

Lipid—fat

Mercantile—a place where the purchase or trade of goods is performed, a store.

Migrate—to go from one country, region, or place to another

Molar—a tooth having a broad biting surface adapted for grinding,

Oxen—an adult steer used as a draft animal.

Parasite—an organism that lives on or in an organism of another species, known as the host.

Predator—any animal that hunts another animal for food.

Predominate—to be the stronger or the leader.

Privy—secret, secluded, a act done in secret.

Roost—a perch upon which birds rest, especially at night.

Ruminate—to chew.

Rupture—to break or to burst.

Secrete—to discharge.

Thistle—any various prickly, composite plants having showy, purple flower heads.

Tranquil—peaceful, quiet, calm.

Treadle—a lever or the like worked by continual action of the foot to impart motion to a machine.

Ventilate—to provide with fresh air.

Vigorous—with healthy physical and mental ability.

Vitamin—substances essential for the body to generate normal energy.

Xylitol—a sugar substitute.

CREDITS

The mice used throughout the book are used under license from 123RF.com.
Copyright Vera Kuttelvaserova

The goat eye is used under license from 123RF.com
Copyright Eric Isselee

The flock of migrating bean geese flying in v-formation
is used under license from 123RF.com
Copyright anagram1

Thistle, ivy and duck prints are used under license from clker.com

Paintings are the work of illustrator Paula Zimmerschied

Mice are a part of life on the farm.
How many did you find while reading about the farm and barnyard?

About the Author

Throughout her life, Kelly Hanson has always been in love with animals, particularly farm animals. Because her family was in the military, she was never able to have farm animals and participate in organizations like 4-H or Future Farmers of America due to frequent moves. She always wanted a pony and you could never pull her away from the petting zoo. When she and her husband (also in the military), relocated to Leavenworth, Kansas; she found her calling as "Farmer Kelly" at a local educational farm. While working at this farm, she was able to interact and learn about common farm animals and loved to share information about the animals with the children, teachers and other visitors to the farm.

When she and her husband, had to move again; Kelly began to take agricultural courses at Missouri State University. She is now working with various local farms and organizations to educate those that are unable to have routine interactions with animals. Today, although Kelly lives in a suburban area, she remains active in learning about farming, farming equipment, and animal husbandry. She actively gardens using the help of compositing worms and other sustainable gardening techniques.

She finally did get her "pony," an American Warmblood, which she routinely shows in English Equitation and Hunter Hack. She can be seen at several local shows in the Kansas City area.

www.ingramcontent.com/pod-product-compliance
Lightning Source LLC
Chambersburg PA
CBHW042029150426
43199CB00002B/12